BLUE

By Patricia M. Stockland
Illustrated by Julia Woolf

Content Consultant
Susan Kesselring, MA
Literacy Educator and Preschool Director

(COLORS)

magic
Wagon

visit us at www.abdopublishing.com

Published by Magic Wagon, a division of the ABDO Publishing Group, 8000 West 78th Street, Edina, Minnesota 55439. Copyright © 2009 by Abdo Consulting Group, Inc. International copyrights reserved in all countries. All rights reserved. No part of this book may be reproduced in any form without written permission from the publisher.

Looking Glass Library™ is a trademark and logo of Magic Wagon.

Printed in the United States.

Text by Patricia M. Stockland
Illustrations by Julia Woolf
Edited by Jill Sherman
Interior layout and design by Nicole Brecke
Cover Design by Nicole Brecke

Library of Congress Cataloging-in-Publication Data

Stockland, Patricia M.
  Blue / by Patricia M. Stockland ; illustrated by Julia Woolf.
     p. cm. — (Colors)
  ISBN 978-1-60270-256-1
  1. Blue—Juvenile literature. 2. Color—Juvenile literature. I. Woolf, Julia, ill. II. Title.
  QC495.5.S772 2009
  535.6—dc22

                                          2008001610

Dad packs our beach bag.

The beach bag is blue.

I wear my best swimsuit.

The swimsuit is blue.

Dad lays down a soft blanket.

The blanket is blue.

8

We look at the big ocean.

The ocean is blue.

I wave to a sailboat.

The sailboat is blue.

We watch the wide sky.

The sky is blue.

Dad spots a small bird.

The bird is blue.

I scoop sand with a pail.

The pail is blue.

I rest under an umbrella.

The umbrella is blue.

I look at Dad's eyes.

His eyes are blue.

What Is Blue?

There are three primary colors: red, blue, and yellow. These colors combine to create other colors. You cannot make the color blue by mixing other colors. You can make blue darker or lighter by adding black or white.

Primary Colors

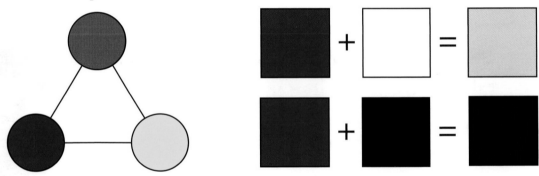

Some colors seem cool. Others seem warm. What colors remind you of a warm fire? What about a cool lake? What blue things did you see in the story? Does blue seem warm or cool to you? Blue is a cool color!

Words to Know

blanket—a soft, warm covering.

pail—a container with a handle.

scoop—to pick something up quickly.

umbrella—a fabric shade that blocks the rain or the sun.

Web Sites

To learn more about the color blue, visit ABDO Publishing Company on the World Wide Web at **www.abdopublishing.com**. Web sites about the colors are featured on our Book Links page. These links are routinely monitored and updated to provide the most current information available.